© 2010 Marlon J McGowan

Published by Jah X-El Publications

Edited and Formatted by Michelle A McGregor

Printed in the United States of America

All rights reserved. No part of this publication may be reproduced, stored in a retrieval system, or transmitted in any form or by any means – for example, electronic, photocopy, recording, etc. – without the prior written permission of the publisher.

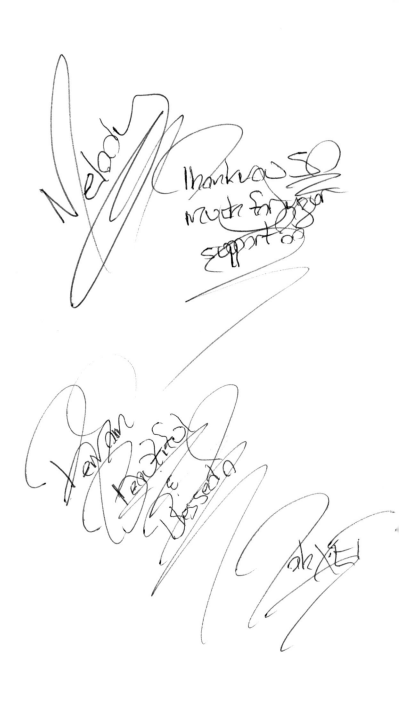

Melody

Thank you so much for your support

Jan Pin

*God **HAS** been, and **WILL** be, the way for **ALL** my achievements **AND** possibilities...*

*...I **CAN'T** express enough thanks, appreciation, and love for what His meaning and worth in my life is to me!!!*

# Table of Contents

## Chapter 6

## Chapter 7

# *Jah'isms II*

# The Variety Volume

Dig... "Truth speak, children **SELDOM** misquote you... In fact, they USUALLY repeat **WORD FOR WORD** what **YOU** should **NOT** have said... So **PLEASE** mind your mouth in their midst..."
~ Jah X-El

# *Reflective Intermission 1*

Dig... "If you're reading this, thank God... You **DON'T** have to be reading this!!!
**THANK GOD**!!!" ~ Jah X-El

# Chapter 1

# *Personal Reflections*

# "The Re-Introduction of Jah"

Allow me to
re-introduce
myself

My name
is Jah

And I've seen
turbulence
and turmoil

Trials and
Tribulations

In my life
I've seen
it **ALL**, and
tested was
my patience

I roamed
the wilderness
of the
hood, lost
for forty
days and
forty nights

Multiplied by

forty-five
and that's nearly
12 years of
my life

That was
at 13, which
took me
to 25, and
since then
there has
been 13
more years
of strife

But through it all I thank God

He sheltered
me inside a pod

Now today
I'm a seed
that's sprouting,
and no matter
how hard
life becomes
from henceforth,
or if the
burden it gives
weigh a ton,

## I **KNOW** I
## **WON'T** fold

I am Jah

And I
am God's
chosen one

He chose me
for an
immeasurably
tough job

And at times
it gets difficult
and really hard

Writing about
problems,
worldly issues,
temptations,
and scandals

Expressing poetic
understanding and
solutions for the
trials, tribulations,
and adversities
that sometimes
seem unmanageable

But I am Jah

And He places
**NOTHING** on
my plate that
as a man
and poet, I
can't handle

He chose me
to sleepwalk
and then
wake up
to see that
He does
have a plan

He chose me
to utilize my
gift and
pen thoughts
poetically in
a way few
men can

He chose
me to
be **ME**

Jah

Now each
day I grow
more patient,
more strong

More wisdom
filled and
knowledgeable
from experiencing
life's rights
**AND** wrongs

Bring on
any challenge!!!

I'm God's
chosen one

Jah

# "From Muse To Masterpiece"

My body

...It
was once
a muse

Now it's
a **MUSE**um
of cuts
and
bruises...

...Abuse
was the
brush

He stroked
on the
pallet of
my frame
a portrait
of hate...

...I
suppose
it a**MUSE**d
his inner
beast

So I,
he beat...

Relentlessly

...Until a
child became
his living
masterpiece

# "No Longer A Masterpiece"

I picture me,
when my thoughts
were like this...

...A convict who's
now irrelevant

The potential to
give **MY** gifts
now extinguished...

...The adroitness
within me that
made **ME** a
masterpiece has been
buried beneath

Steal, bars,
and concrete...

...And minds
psyched to think

That their artistic
thoughts are
now obsolete...

...I too, **WAS**

a masterpiece
For **YEARS** on
lock, I felt
my existence
totaled irrelevancy...

...Couldn't dream
beyond mint green

That was the
hue of the walls
surrounding me...

...Being mentally
fed by
convicts stories

Of what
USED to be...

...When they
were in
"*The World*"
and who they
**USED TO BE**

How they
**WERE**, at
one time,
a masterpiece...

...A vision
that's quickly
becoming blurry

Fading...

...Especially...

...When it's
**"COUNT TIME"**,
**"LIGHTS OUT"**,
and it's pitch
black that's
my surrounding

CO's making
rounds, counting...

...Whistling and
keys jiggling

Dead bolts and
air locks turning...

...Inmates rushing
to fall asleep
Hurriedly...

...Trying to get
to **THAT** dream

Where they're
once again
a masterpiece...

...But I **BELIEVED**

I **KEPT** alive the thought that freedom **WASN'T**
just a fantasy...

...I **WOULD**
be free

But it was a
distant reality...

...Easily immured
in this depressed,
oppress dwelling

So even while
locked up I
held on to
my artistry...

...And I
kept writing

And Ms. Poetry
kept supporting...

...Throughout my
**ENTIRE** bid, she
stayed with me

Faithfully…

...Unconditionally

Her presence
in my life allowed
me to pen heaven
when there was
**NOTHING** but
hell around me...

...Ever heard a
grown man crying?

Witnessed a
fatal stabbing?

...Took a shower
while next to
you there
was a man's
body hanging?

Sometimes **ALL**
**IN THE SAME**

**DAY**, and **THIS**
is daily living...

...Where dudes
doing life **NO**
**LONGER** remember
when they were
a masterpiece

Because you lose
focus in prison,
**YOU LOSE**
**YOUR LIFE**, so
they can't afford
to waste thoughts
on what is
now, a
meaningless thing...

...That's that
incarcerated
mentality

I've been there,
and on **THIS**,
I can
**TRULY** speak...

...When you
**KNOW** you're
**BETTER** than

what the
prosecutor deemed
When you **KNOW**
you're **NOT** as
ugly as the
jury was
convinced to see...

...When you
**KNOW** your
worth is **GREATER**
than what
the judge ruled
you to be...

When **ALL** you
wanted to scream
was "**ONLY**
**GOD CAN**
**JUDGE ME**"!!!

...But you
were **STILL**
found guilty

At **THAT**
moment losing
your status as
a masterpiece...

No longer
a rarity...

...Just 1 of a
countless many

No longer free...

...No longer
a product
of ingenuity

No longer
artistry...

...No longer
a masterpiece

# "Hill Top Memories"

...I found
my home
on that hill

In that
dry heat
of Orlando...

...Under those
fading faithful clouds

Where I desired to
be in the white
snow of Michigan's
December...

...My
mentality on that
pedestal
of dirt rang
with memories

Of yellow
spots and blue
signatures...

...Those bed sheets...

...In the back of my mind...

...At 15
remembering shining

The
Lyrical Lord
battle rapping...

...Annihilating

Also crying
while writing...

Pain obtruding Joy

...Because
when I penned,
a youthful
world of
abuse I
was escaping

That's why
Spectators and
adversary's would
sometimes see tears
while I was rhyming...

...Yes, I
found my home on

this hill

This enormous
place of solitude
and serenity...

...Dried and rock
infested

Colored only
by the
tracks of
my sneakers
laid dirty steps...

...Struggling to breathe
in labored
breaths

Tired is
how I felt...

**NOT** appropriate

...That a child
should have to
feel like this

...old…

Standing there on
top of my ageless,
fantastical home...

...Positively
cursing the
wind and debris
passing

For catapulting
me into
reminiscing...

...When as
a preteen,
I contemplated
a self-imposed
early ending

I wept
in a whole
new chapter...

...Placing my mark
and love on
my castle

That was
my last place
of efface and
seclusion...

Paradise

...There

Transfixed in
felicity and
misery on
what I
know **NOW**,
was a
paradoxical
hill that
gave **ONLY**
an intoxicating
illusion…

# "When I Write
## (*The Love*[*Less*] *Chronicle*)"

When I write
I can be
a hieroglyph
hibernating in
your heart

I can become
a hermit in your
luminous laugh

I can paint
picture's in
pastel that
are enriched
in love and
brightens your
day in the dead
of the night

I can coast
through your
dreams like
a swan
on passions
hazy lake

I can have

you staring
at me
with intoxicating
brown eyes that
sift through a
man's soul
like powdered
sugar sprinkled
from the skies
raining down in
the form of
celestial kisses

With my poetry,
I can show
you how
to love again

But apparcntly
I'm destined
to be alone
and loveless...

So love for
me, I can't
poetically pen

When I verbalize
what I write

I can excoriate
your burdens
with my tongue

Orally replace
them with wings

Have you flying
when I divide
your thighs with
my linguistics

Lyrical cunnilingus

Have you
orgasmically
floating

Climatically
Soaring

When I write
I can till the
soil where he
has buried
your heart

Prepare it for
a growth of
abundant love

...Yes, I **KNOW** he has you waiting...

He has you
emotionally
stagnate

In the
*Rolls Royce*
mind-state

Love doesn't
reside within
you anymore

So you choose
to wait on
the day when
you can trust
and love again,
but waiting on
that day sometimes
feel like waiting
on "*Leap Year*"
to come back
around after
it **JUST** passed

But when I
write, I can
make you

realize that
you **NEED** to
get back on
the path
of love

The *O' Jays*
destination

Make it possible
for you to
catch loves train

There's no time
like the present

So I present this
present to you

A manuscript
to inspire
and assure

Just leave me
with a token of
your appreciation
for the lovely
speck of light
I'm awakening
with this scribe

Remind **ME**

Tell me
that there's
love out there,
**SOMEWHERE**,
for Jah

Because with my
poetry, I can
show **YOU** how
to love again

But apparently
**I'M** destined
to be alone
and loveless...

So love for **ME**,
I can **NOT**
poetically pen

# "Schizo Insight
## (*Jah Reflecting On And Motivating Jah*)"

...I saw a
ribbon today

Because of
it, I'm now
glancing @
my past
through my
intellectual
looking glass...

...Thoughts
shattered into
/s/h/a/r/d/s
of regret

Slivers of my
mind reflecting
on doctor's
revelations
in retrospect...

**ALAS**!

...Jah is
assaulted with
a maniacal
mosaic of

medical defects

///mental///clock//moving/
//backwards///

::((tock))::((tick))::

I see
burgundy ribbons...

...Inherited glitches

Being told
of present
sicknesses...

...Oh, the
memories

Being told I'm
ill had me
amused and
full of misery...

...In front of
the *Medical
Man* having a
4 minute nervous
breakdown
and going

momentarily crazy

One day
you're well,
then the next
you have
numerous
life altering,
threatening
ailing(s)...

...Physically fit
externally, but
internally
you're failing

These natural
"*Fuck You's!*"
have come
from 75%
genetic
mistakes...

...19%
recycled
heartache

6% of
"*Those Are
The Breaks*"...

...A shudder
or two

Stutter-step
and life
comes unglued...

...There's a
reason this
replica of
a man is
now scaled
down to size

Hypertension
combined
with an aortic
aneurysm...

**-Demise Realized-**

*...This is how
I may die*!?

Burgundy
ribbons
visualized...

...Makes me
reminiscence

about when
death crept

Sneak, theft, then
left...

...Wife lost
as sudden
as an inhale
of breath

Beautiful head
laid at rest...

On a crimson
stained
pillow case
and bed
spread...

...Maroon
visions

Cause of death:
Brain Aneurysm...

...Cause ribbons

Burgundy
reflections...

...Saturate my
sight and flood
my mind

But the will
to rebuild and
live is mine...

...No "*Pity Parties*"
or crying

No self loathing
at times...

...The **ONLY**
thing left for
me to do
is **SHINE**
Jah, **SIIINE**!!!

## "Poets Pity Party"

The battle for
**US** is never-ending

WE have fought
so long to
become peddlers
of dreams

Remitters of
past lives

Inexhaustible
swimmers
in
the
sea of thought

Indefatigable
runners
on
the
land
of
imagination

Tireless
fliers
in
the

sky
of
creativity

Dramatic embracers
of the gentle verse

Still

**WE** fall prey
to the compromising

To the **UN**compromising

Sometimes conveniently
forgetting to romanticize

**QUICK** to criticize

Our **EVERY** breath
that manifest into
poetic scribes

Under the fading
Venetian sunset
to the waters
that line the
coast of California
to the dusty
landscape of Africa

to the skyline
of New York
to the polluted
atmosphere of
the moon

## STILL

**WE** remain impatient
to meet in countless,
infinite, endless
places, sources for
poetic fuel

Poetical Fools

**WE** seem to
be to the outside
world that has
**NO** sympathy nor
understanding of
what it's like
to be haunted
and possessed by
the "*gift*" of
lyrical expression

The constant written
and unwritten letters

The verbalized

and silent thoughts

Vowing nevermore

Never again

**NEVER**

Will **WE** put
into versed writing
what you **ALL**
seemingly can't!!!

But **WE** *CAN'T*

**WE** birth
more poems

Demigods of
structured,
rhythmical
compositions

Trying to scribe
immortality with
our literary work

Scribing for
**OURSELVES**

Unrealistic reasons
to believe **WE
WILL**, but realistically
knowing our thoughts
*may*, last beyond
the dates of social
celebration and
historical time lines

Remember **US**!!!!!

.....*sigh*.....

Futile

Dig... "Truth speak, we **ALL**, at times, become weak... But one should **NEVER** say you hate life; that's extremely close to blasphemy... I mean **SERIOUSLY**!!! How does an individual curse or feel negative about having received the gift of **LIFE**, which is from God, an immeasurably divine **BLESSING**!? We human beings take for granted that we are **LIVING**... Truth speak, we **DON'T** have to be!!!" ~ Jah X-El

# *Reflective Intermission 2*

Dig... "Truth speak, just because an individual is experienced **DOESN'T** mean they're wise... Just like an individual being older **DOESN'T** mean they're mature... **NO**!!! An individual does **NOT** become wise just because they've had experiences... **NOT**!!! That's why some life experiences are repeated... An individual becomes wise by not only **LEARNING** from, but **APPLYING** the wisdom gained from experiences..." ~ Jah X-El

# Chapter 2

## *Encouragement*

# "A Week And A Half Later"

After all is
said and done

He returned
expecting
everything
in place

In the land
of make
believe he
didn't break
your heart
in two…

…and

All is
right when
it comes
to you...

…and

You will
accept it
because
you should...

...be the
one to
want love
no matter
the condition...

...and

Pure distinction
between selfish
and selfless

After all is
said and done

You have
exhaled a
relief that
you held as you
carried the
relationship

Exhausted from
little affection

Hoping to
reach the
oasis where
he'll realize
what you

offer is...

...Priceless

(*Useless*)

After all is
said...

...You **SHOULD**
be **DONE**!!!

# "So You Wanna Be A Baby Mama???"

Another girl lost

Turned out and
exploited by business suits

White tee's and skinny jeans

Tapers, fades, locs, and braids

We need to be more conscious of
how our daughters are raised

Righteous steps

Stress vocabulary

Begin with "*Like-A-Lady*"

How they should carry

Don't pick up committing sins

All too easy when coming in contact
with well developed men

Then becoming a-**DICK**-ted to the thickness
they're carrying

Mentality needs to grow

Separate loving her
from just fucking her

Try teaching her

To guard herself from a handcuff marriage

And **NOT** settling with an insecure warden
just to say that she's married

Don't be a burial ground

Consisting of random dude diggers whose
ambition was just to bury male bone in
her feminine ground

I seen plenty

*Breathless Beauties*

*Bodacious Bodies*

*Lite & Pretty*

*Dark & Lovely*

**ALL** with **NO** self esteem

Personality and character ugly

Loud in public, drinking publicly

And women drunk are horrifying

Their lush-like behavior lead them into
horizontal promises that they're keeping

Last night's spectacle

The next morning feeling like a sperm receptacle

That's why their weekends are famous for one
night stands

They don't know that they're nicknamed
"Ms. Luther Vandross" by ignorant motherfuckers

"*If Only For One Night*"
wishes **ALWAYS** come true with her

So that makes them truthful motherfuckers

And she, a stupid woman who allows ignorant
motherfuckers to fuck her

Creating possible riots in clubs with men **AND**
at home with her children

Because she's **THERE** and **NOT** "*there*"; get it?

Life scarred,
vicious cycle

She's one multiple mistake making madam

Never learning from making multiple mistakes
of letting miscellaneous men ride in her saddle

Future plans?

Idle

Erase intelligent dreams of being a doctor or
lawyer

Was ambitious...

...back when she painted pictures

of being a lovely main squeeze quest...

Ended up being an idiotic man's conquest

A fantasy accomplished

She allowed it, so that made her an idiotic
accomplice

Made her a young nigga's dream come true

Allowed him to take you

Babymama you

Then left you

Alone, crying like your baby and more responsible

Cleaning doo doo

Periodically feeling like doo doo

### *BOO HOO*

Get over it Boo Boo

Real **LADIES** get married while easy individuals
in your species
remain solo

Freeze frame these words in your brain like a
photo

They're wisdom of profit

Stop it

Being just another baby mama investment

Being just a commode for disrespect

Connect to the higher class product you are

instead of being just another low class female
object

## "Letters + Numbers"

He had ten
fingers with
only five
that produce

She had
nine questions
of "**WHY**!?"
that lay
beneath the
surface of her
beautiful but
battered head

There are
now eight
breaks in
a heart
that no
longer beat
the way
it should

She said
seven honest
words that
say nothing
but the truth

## (**Get The Fuck Out Of My Life**)

Six times
he made
three word
noises that
didn't even
make sense

(*I Love You*, but mumbled incoherently)

She allowed
his hands to
question her
five times...

## **TWICE**...

Trying to
get an
answer that
doesn't exist

Four
incompetent
tries to
breathe
breath
into a long

dead and
deteriorating
relationship

She tried
three that
were holy

And he was
**ALREADY**
two inches
too short

And one
time, I
asked her
the **REAL**
question

*"Lady...?*

*How many
times will
you attempt
to use
numbers
to explain
the
unutterable?"*

Your chest

cavity can't
utter the
words that
your spirit
mumbles
though

...Too many
chances
you're giving
this dude...

No matter
how much
you struggle
through
algebraic
numbers in
hopes that
this formula
will produce

Your numbers
and his words
don't add up
to nothing
but abuse

That's
the truth

His lovingly
vicious vowels,
noun, verbs,
and syllables
that are
meant for
your ears,
always end
up wrapped
around your
your neck

But I'll give
you a 2
word, 10
letter, algebra
formula that
will solve this

**A B U S E** = **L E A V E**

**THAT'S** the
**ONLY**
equation that
make sense
to me

Truth speak

You can run

square roots
into logic
until you've
created some
sort of
excuse
for this

But your
numbers and
his numbers
were **NEVER**
meant to mix

So

Ten is the
number of
fingers that
grace
your hands
when you
put them
together

Nine multiplied
by never-ending
is the
amount of
times your

knees touch
the ground
in prayer

Eight times
infinite
represents
the moments
your soul is
freed through
ten fingers

Seven are
the
miscellaneous
gifts of his
you wish
to return

But six are
the amount
of times I'll
tell you that's
shit you
should throw
away, pawn,
or burn

Remember,
his five hurt
when they

touched you

Four of
those he
said he
was sorry

(He wasn't, but he **REALLY** is)

Three of
those he
said he
loved you

(He didn't, and he **NEVER** did)

Two is the
number of
times you
believed him

One

Is all it
takes ladies

He put his
hands on
you once;
**LEAVE HIM**!

## "Tattoo"

Here you
are a woman

But standing
before him,
simply a girl

And this is
why I said
before that
you should
be a
**TRUE** lady

Not a "*sweetie*"

Infinitely more
than a "*baby*"

**DEFINITELY NOT**
his "*mommy*"

As grown as
he "*should*" be

Dig... If you're
allowing an adult

man to call
you "mommy"
then you
**DESERVE** to be
treated as a
child; he may
as well be
your daddy

If you **DON'T**
understand that,
you **BOTH**
need therapy

And you
contemplate why
he mistreats and
see's you as fake

…or flawed

...and **ALWAYS**
misunderstood

You are a
mound of
sticky labels

But in a few
seconds, after

he dismisses
you for another
misses you will
be a blur
of proof that
you are trapped

If you were
a tattoo, you
would be
on his back

Hidden from sight,
and like he
wants you,
playing the back

Can you see
past this
ingenious trap?

Or do you
remain stagnant
at the revolving
door of women
walking over his
welcome mat?

Or are
you a new
prefix now?

An "*ex*"?

Or "*meta*" to
his physical
only when
he wants
you for sex

The misuse
of his eyes

It's the
ultimate
interference
with his
"*masculine*"
condition

How are **YOU**
tattooed in his
mind and viewed
in his vision?

# "Woman, I Can Solve Your Loneliness"
## (*An Inspirational Reminder*)

You're a
rendition of
beauty that
has yet to
be defined
with diction

You will **NOT**
find your
name in
lights above
the crowd,
awaiting
performance,
for you
excel on a
deeper level

You transcend
**ALL** Queens
who sat on
the throne
before you

So why do
you run
amok and
allow to

bother you,
the worst
of solitude?

All along
straying off
of your
preparation
path to
a well
deserved crown?

A crown
meant for
**YOUR**
exact fit

But know **THIS**

A mere
"*woman*" isn't
worthy of a
**LADY'S** royal
head-dress

Fortunately, my
writes allow
you to
travel near
for insight

instead of
traveling far
for the
chance to
never regret

Dig...

If you're
alone, then
**SO BE IT**

You'd rather
be alone with
a feeling
of **SELF
TOGETHERNESS**,
than to
be gathered
with a
multitude of
manipulative men
and endure
the loneliness
of their
judging crowd

But is this it?

Is this
miserable and

lonely place
within you
meant to
be your
vintage palace?

So many
rooms in
your head, so
much space
in your heart,
yet, **ONE**
peon of
a man
resides there

How can
you be
a leader of
your feelings
when you
are emotionally
being misled?

Chasing the
love of
a man who
treats you
wrongly with
**NO** respect?

That would
make you
a follower
of games
and B.S.

And I would
much rather
have you
loving **YOU**
more than
you love
him instead

So woman,
the 3 words
in the next
sentence, you
should trust...

You're
**ANYTHING** but

**ONLY** because
your mind isn't
right is why
you don't have
an army of
soldiers gathered
for the battle
of your heart

Nor do you
confidently
come into
a domain
with male
supporters of
your happiness
ready to listen

You have
not even
issued your
first **REAL**
relationship
want, desire,
or need
from a man

Well, this
of **YOU**,
I command

This of **YOU**,
I **DEMAND**

It's time for
**YOU** to take
**YOUR** rightful
appointment

Woman, **YOU**
are royalty
by birthright

Heiress
by promise

Know **YOURSELF**
as *Queen*

Love the
temple that
is **YOU**

Take **YOUR**
place on
the throne

If my poems
teach you
women **NOTHING**
else, they
**SHOULD** remind
you that when
you carry
yourself as
**MORE** than
a mere woman...

A magnificent
**LADY**...

The **LEAST** of
your worries
will be about
being alone...

## "Reflection"

Sometimes
we must
stop and
admire
the small
things...

The sunrise,
the sunset,
a star,
the moon,
a flower...

"**YOU**", my
cherished
friends...

The smile of
a child...

The hello
of a
stranger or
just a
passer by...

The song

of a bird...

A poem
tender as
this one
or as
passionate
as a dream...

Sometimes
we must
block the
evil and
the pain,
the
hopelessness,
the hate
and
**ALL** things,
circumstances,
and situations
that bring
adversity

And...

Let love
flow in

And...

Teach us

Endow us
with wisdom
from our
turbulent
past...

Then apply
that wisdom
so that we
won't travel
those roads
of conflict
again

And...

Fill our
hearts with
the sweet
perfume of
a fresh
morning dew
and a
bright new
beginning...

# "These 2 Words"

They're seldom considered,
though they do more to
influence everything
about one than virtually
any two things in a life...

They often control the time
one gets up in the morning,
the time one goes to sleep,
what one eats and drinks
and the very thoughts that
run through their head...

They can make one either
happy or sad, loving or
hateful, cheerful or
remorseful, congenial
or spiteful, and in doing
so, control the very capacity
that one has for success...

No, one doesn't often think
of them, instead one **BLAMES**
the problem it creates on
the shortcoming of others,
or the state of the
economy, or on family,
or a million other reasons...

Often, at times, unable to
find anyone or anything
else to **BLAME**, one looks
for shortcomings within
themselves on which
to lay the **BLAME**...

When their impact on ones
life is fully considered, in
one's every thought and
action, when one is mindful
of their awesome power,
when one nurtures and
groom's them for positive
use in their lives, they
can become more contagious
than the most prolific disease
ever witnessed by man...

Their influence **WILL** spread
to every person they
come in contact with...

Groomed and nurtured in
a positive manner, there
**WILL** be **NO** person or
obstacle that can stand
in the way of their
success, or fail to be
impacted for the better...

They are *Attitudes* and *Belief*

.

Dig... "Truth speak, if **ALL** you contributed to your children was the sperm it took to conceive them, then you **SHOULDN'T** even be considered a "*Sperm Donor*"... A **TRUE** sperm donor serves a purpose; you **DON'T**... You **SHOULD** be considered a "*Sperm Defect*" because **REAL MEN** are responsible, therefore **YOUR** daddy's sperm was lacking in potency and complete male attributes dude..." ~ Jah X-El

# *Reflective Intermission 3*

Dig... "Truth speak, if **YOU** place a low value on **YOURSELF**, you can be **ASSURED** your worth will **NOT** be raised by the world around you... Truth speak, you **SHOULDN'T** place a value on yourself **ANYWAY**... Be **PRICELESS!!!**"
~ Jah X-El

# Chapter 3

# *Spiritual*

## "Comfort Food"

Maybe that
dude and
sugar made
her crazy...

...But I never
heard of a
woman claiming
glucose insanity

And I guess
all her "*girl's*"
around her
got a contact
high from her
sugar smack...

...Cause I swear,
with the "*advice*"
they give,
considering the
"*boys*" they
have in
**THEIR** lives,
they too
have lost
their minds

But nevertheless,

she's possessed
by stress...

...Or more
of a lack
of chocolate
covered kisses

She misses
the sweetness
of piece...

...Yes, **PIECE**,
not peace

A piece
of a man...

...Because of
this, she
can't sleep

She doesn't
want to
sleep anyway
because her
want for
a man
will occupy
her dreams...

...So she seeks
solace for her
state of mind
with a bowl
of creamy mint
chocolate chip
ice cream

With a cone...

...In a dish

Or straight
out the
box until
the quart
is gone...

...And **THEN**
her lack
of sleep
wake up her
cravings for
greens and
hot water
corn bread

Not the
average 2 am
snack food...

...Though her
pallet desires
kindness and
consideration

A man's
administrations
and admiration's...

...Her stomach
settles for tasty
treats that pack
pounds and
inevitably lead
to other
bad vices
and negative
consumptions

On her thighs
and waistline,
the calories
will stick...

...But she would
much rather
have masculine
hands clutching
and clinging
to her hips

His lips
embracing
her lips...

...She wants
to be
sweetly kissed

But there's no
man around
so she goes
to the fridge...

...She'll attempt
to replace that
desire with a
sugary glass
of ice cold
lemonade to sip

And the 100
calorie snacks
**STILL** won't
satisfy her craving
for companionship...

...So she has
been eating
up attention
from ex's

Various men
who are little
more than randoms
and miscellaneous'...

...She won't lie

She has
dreams of
a life luxurious
and extravagant...

...Now she's
awakening to a
reality different

A life
only fulfilling
in weight
and decadent...

...**TOTALLY** altered
from the life she
once perceived

Her views
changed because
he was cheating...

...And the taste

of betrayal
is still bitter

And she thinks...

*"As fresh
as the
morning dew,
his wrongs
sit upon
my tongue,
taunting me"*

Greedy?

...No, her food
addiction only
hits her when
she's needy

So what then
becomes of
the scripture
in Corinthians?

...10:31 doesn't
quite apply to
this situation

*"Whether you
eat or drink,*

*whatever you
do, do so
to the glory
of God*"

...No, 10:31 in
relation to
this is odd

Because she
doubts that
her binges
glorify anything
but her thighs...

...Yet, she's
found it
quite difficult
to control
cravings for
comfort foods

No wonder
why migraines
have returned
to wreck havoc
on her brain...

...And she
doesn't mind

the temporary
escape provided
by that
occasional
stint of pain

Because **THAT**
pain takes away
from "*not having
a man*" pain...

...But to make
it all plain

She wants to
be happy again...

...And I **KNOW**
that she can

So here's
**MY** suggestion...

...Instead of
seeking the
serenity of
a Snickers
tonight to
send her
to sleep

She should
stay on her
knees praying
until out of
her mind, his
presence creeps...

...Maybe a fast
is needed to
break the
stronghold of
loneliness
and grief

No need to
eat for relief...

...It's deliverance
she seeks

And she's weak...

...So she needs
to hear from
God to be
filled with
encouragement
and
strength
spiritually

Because while
digesting earthly
tasty treats...

...His voice
is muffled

Mumbled
and distorted...

...Contorted

That's the
extent of her
vision while
in such
a condition...

...Maybe that
dude and
sugar **HAS**
made her
crazy, but
His Word
will make
her whole

She needs
the food

from "***The Man Above***"
to fill her soul..

## "Saved & Sexy"

Pour me
spiritual, lyrical
sweetness

From out
of a
chocolate
colored
cover bible

Sweet

I keep a
sweet tooth
for Godly
consciousness

Poetically, I
can spoil you

When it
comes to
you, I
can't help
but pen
my passion
for your
seasoned with
sweetness

soul food

You're a habit

Easily, to
you, I'm addicted

You're a
*Diseased Diva*,
you spread spiritual
sickness, and
with **YOU**,
I'm **GLADLY**
inflicted

Lady, with you
I'm infected

That's why I
now vomit
love rhetoric

God is
a genius

Who else
can wrap beauty,
brains, and
**BAAAD** bodies in
an abundance

and variety
of feminine packages

He enabled
she's to go
from scripture
studiers to
sex symbols

From ministers
to models

The inspiration
for these
poetic syllables

And even
thugs who
pop bottles

She's called
a religious fanatic

I call her
a hopeless romantic

Because she's
limitless in
her love

Sometimes

to her own detriment

Oftentimes
adoring Jesus
as much as
she adores
male scrubs,
with their anti-christ
like antics

But she's
**STILL** a
woman of
greatness

And **NOT**
a follower
of satan

And **NOT**
"wordly"

And **NO**
dummy

In the race
for irrelevant
satanic
followers,
she's **NOT**

in the running

She's a
peer pressure
rejecter

Prime example
of following
Christ reflector

*Divine*
*Soul Sister*

*Spiritual*
*Gift Giver*

Up lifter

Encourager

*Sanctified Soldier*

*Prayer Warrior*

*God's Desired*
*Daughter*

Avid supporter

Of The Almighty,
and His

ALL Knowing word

And since
she's not
perfect,
sometimes
of unworthy
men, and
their absurd
blurbs

She's
simultaneously
blessed and
highly favored

Lusted after
and highly
desired

Saved
and sexy

Carries herself
Honestly

Obedient and
Trustworthy

Dedicated

girlfriend
and clergy

A member
of the *Body
of Christ*

With a body
that's **NICE**

Stacked, fat,
thick, thin,
skinny,
it's **ALL** right!

**ALL** the
time angelic

Character
**ALWAYS**
charismatic

Personality
**ALWAYS**
magnetic

A **LADY**
who's
**ALWAYS**
respected

Men are
**ALWAYS**
attracted

Spiritual women
are **FANTASTIC**

## "Oaths"

We make **BOTH** without contemplation

Fun to conceive but hard to deliver

Our promises are like babies

Dig... "Ladies, if you find that people call/label you **FEMINIST** because you're direct in speech, firm in your beliefs, and don't bend to the whims of men or societies demands, or when you express thoughts that differentiate you from a doormat, prostitute, or woman who's easily misused/mistreated, then **TRUST ME**, you're doing something **RIGHT** and "*they*" hate independence and strength in a feminine form!"

~ Jah X-El

# *Reflective Intermission 4*

Dig... "Beauty, handsomeness, and **ALL** things attractive are meant to be seen... If not, God wouldn't have blessed us with the gift of sight... But he **ALSO** enabled us with the gift of reasoning, will, and decision making, and sometimes, as human beings, we allow our vision to make bad choices for us..." ~ Jah X-El

# Chapter 4

# *Ode to Poetry*

## "Ageless Love"

...You give
me anything
that my
heart desires

And I treat
each moment
with you
like antiques...

...And never
again will
my gray
hair make
me feel
embarrassed

Despite the
silver that's
beginning to
become
sneaky and
peek through
the black...

...With you,
I **NEVER** have
to worry or

wonder about
my wrinkles

With you,
I'm **NEVER**
ashamed of them...

...These newly
defined lines
upon my skin

Un-hidden...

...Tell tale
signs of wisdom

Evidence of
natural development
movements emerging
from deep within...

...Written accounts of
the transition from youth
to middle age expressed
through my manuscripts

I embrace and adore
the reasons for my
possession of
crows feet...

...And you don't waste
time trying to confirm
to me my youth

As if fresh age hasn't
quite started to fade yet...

...No lies,
I know
I'm mature...

...Becoming
older

But I, you
still adore...

...And with
you, I
forget newly
discovered
years of
creaky bones
as daily laughter
erupts from
deep in my soul

And
manifest...

# POETRY

...Thank you
for loving me

Regardless of
my subsequent
seniority...

# "Muse[sic] N Poetry"

I call
her my
Charlie Parker

Whisperer to
the birth
of the
star in me

Of melancholy
and inspired
spirit

Lost behind
the gray
side of perfection

I call her
my Col "trane"

Sends chills
up my
spine that
keep me
moving along
the lyrical
railways

My Billie
Holiday of
sensual
distraction

Makes me
prolific in
words with
her gorgeous
songs

Breathed in
and exhaled
her lessons

Received a
beautiful
inception

Jah, you
can be Master
of Manuscripts

I call
her my
Miles Davis

Blowing true
and wondrous
as a

Jah X-El

mornings dew

Leaving me
speechless
and
challenged

And so
I call
her

Poetic Promise

Of rhythm
and roses

Covered
tenderly
with faith
and passion

Written
incredibly so

I call
her my
jazz and
rhythm

Without a

113

**REAL**
description

**SO** very
complicated

Politely
nicknamed
"Muse"

Because poems
exists within
the music
which is
her voice

And for
it all, I
call her

Poetry

# "Ear'gasms (*The Reunion*)"

You're about
to witness
a reunion

Where words
meet minds

Karma sutric
poetry will
be born

A poetic
baby will
be birthed
from this
erotic fusion

It's been a
long time

Allow me
to remind

...Again...

Allow me
to deliver
remembrances

of what
verbal ecstasy
feels like for
your brain

Allow me
to slide
inside your
mind and
drip thoughts
into the
cracks and
fissures
of your
sensually
stimulated
membranes

Let my
spoken
word lick
your thought
processes

Leaving you
breathless

Leave you
dripping wet
from my
metaphoric mists

Have you
saying

"Jah, shower
your lyrics
over me..."

"This is the
place I
**ALWAYS**
want to be..."

Sweet Epiphany

The spot
where
beautiful
minds meet

And I'm
giving a
110 percent
effort,
lyrically
breaking
your back
when I
dive deep

Mentally

Torrential
ear'gasms
will be
exploding
from
your pysche

And I'll
continue
penetrating

Thrusting
poetry

Reminding
you of
what my
poetic sutra
feels like
between
"these"

# "Let's Make Love (*The Amalgamation*)"

I saw you
watching me

Visually calling
out to me

Asking for
my hand
in marriage

You were blank

Empty before
I came along

Wanting to
be touched
by my thoughts

My ideas

My words

So, into
existence,
became our
amalgamation

Such a
joyful
consolidation

And now
we solidify
our union
with the
consummation
of my pen

Making love
to all your
sweet pages

My thoughts
become tattoos
of priceless
art filling
the voids
of your body

Every inch
of you
becomes a
part of me
as my ink
spills and
impregnates you

Instantly giving
birth to
a beautiful
baby called

Poetry

And now I
share our
first child
with the
world with
the anticipation
of creating
more siblings

More of
our love
thoughts made
manifest into
rhythmic verse

Poems

So how
about it,
my beautiful,
blank page

My pen

is erect

My mind
is stimulated

Let's make love

Again

Dig... "Truth speak, God has provided **US**, and the world we live in, with **ALL** the things we need to make our lives meaningful... Purposeful... It's up to **US** to maximize our potential... Make our blessings, which is our gifts and talents, useful... Enable ourselves to make living more joyful..."
~ Jah X-El

# *Reflective Intermission 5*

Dig... "Truth speak, it was/is the **IDIOTIC** ignorant, who in their imbecilic ignorance, misuse the word "*ignorant*" in an antagonistic connotation when applying it to some individuals, that the expression was/is made to seem unfavorable... This was/is why the word is widely perceived as negative... **NOT**!!! Educate yourselves **PLEASE**... We were **ALL** ignorant at one time or another..." ~ Jah X-El

# Chapter 5

## *Love Thoughts*

## "I Am Love (*The Assassination*)"

I am love - You **ALL** continuously
welcome me
with open arms

But be forewarned

My reflections are
untimely and rude

Made to enlighten
and insult you dudes

Crude

I can be brash
with sick delivery

Just right for the
physical rat .ta .tat .tat

Flat line your heart
with what's beneath
these lines

No need for
comebacks, I
annihilate with
perfection

No exceptions

I grace no life
without exceptional
direction

Or confusing
misdirection

I am love

I've provided and
given many sighs

I'm deadly

Maneuvering through
the carbon copies
you all call your minds
with incredible color

I'm precise

Try to time me and
I last eternally
in your life

Pain, I bring it
and rip it
with cold blows

and steps

Taking no prisoners
and shitting on what's left

I curse you in whatever
form cause you
stand no different

You all bring plastic
spoons to blade battles
of mind and power

You can't win

I eat you up and spit
you out with disfavor

Leave **THAT** in your
mouth, hearts, and
minds to savor

I am love

I bury the ashes
of the fallen in the
ink of the meaningless
love sonnets I insult you with

I wish I could erase you

Move on to the next
individual who thinks
they're worthy

The talented clergy's
of verse and ballads,
I serve thee

Poets work for me

Pen B.S. that will
have you weak for me

I am love

All respect due
because there
will **NEVER** be
an emotion like me

Until Jah came
along and claimed
me deceased

A lyrical assassin
who composed
my obituary - I *WAS* love

# "Calendar of Love"

I want to
taste you
late Tuesdays

Until you wake
early Wednesdays

Quench your
Thursdays till
Friday

Sit Saturdays
sipping your
Sundays till
Monday

You see I,
want to love
you daily

Seasonally

I want you
to get sprung
from my tongue
in the Spring

Sizzle from

the soliloquies
I'll speak
directly to
your womb
while acting
out our
sexual dramas
in the Summer

Feast on you
until you're
falling, calling
my name as
you and
I anticipate
the cumming
of Autumn

Prepare for
the pleasure
I plan
on providing
you below
the waist
in Winter

My love
is **ALL**
the seasoning
you'll need

I want you
lusting for
me as
I slide
off your
January's

Pull down
your
February's

March right
up in
between
your April's
as your May
becomes
June and
your July
lays naked
in the
August of
my September

Until you
Remember

That October
was when
my naughty

November
first eased
inside your
delicious
December

Listen

All I'm trying
to say is
I want to
love you
continuously

Daily

Monthly

Yearly

In **EVERY** way

Dig... {*The Perfecter In God*} - "Spiritual love **PERFECTS** our sight... It allows us to **NOT** endeavor in the impossible search for "The **PERFECT** *Person*"... Instead, it allows us to see an **IMPERFECT** person **PERFECTLY**... It let's us view their **IMPERFECTIONS** as **PERFECTION**, or simply flaws that make them unique in personality and character when our vision is **PERFECTED** through God!" –

{*The Perfecter In God*} ~ Jah X- El

# *Reflective Intermission 6*

Dig... {*The Choice Is YOURS*} - "Truth speak, the heart often chooses a path... Doesn't mean it has to be followed... Allow the mind to make **THAT** decision..." - {*The Choice Is YOURS*} ~ Jah X-El

# Chapter 6

# *Expressions of Erotica*

## "Cummin' of The Storm"

It all starts with an essence in the air...

...Clouds rolling in

Thickening the atmosphere...

...Ocean currents become waves at first

Quenching the beaches thirst...

...Timid, gentle rains fall

Random lightning flashes...

...Thunder calling

Still lands softly rolling...

...Plateaus shaking

Trees trembling...

...The oceans give way to intuition; release
streaming surges

Winds moaning and howling...

...Quakes releasing their natural, primal urges

Mountains shudder with a **MIGHTY THUNDER**...

...Lava **SPEWING**, flowing as a river

Volcanic lust spilling over...

...Tidal waves and narrowing chasms

The world churns and sputters...

**DISCONNECT**

...And then you reach an **ORGASM**!!!

# "Shared Thoughts of Her"

This morning

Began with
intense
breathing

Candles,
full of
erotic scents

Body sweats

Spots wet

Yes

She, got
me open

Ever since
first talks
with her,
I've been gon'

Romance on
the horn

Pleasurable

sessions with
self shared
on the phone

In person,
we're at war

Our bodies
fluids having
orgasmic shootouts

There's **NEVER**
Losing

We **BOTH** win

End the day and
begin the night with
sunset walks

Continued
with copious
conversation
by the
bedside that
eventually create
pillow talk

I fantasize
of having
fornicating

fun with
my female buddy
of mine

Our moans
being the
instrumental
playing in
the background
during our
adult playtime

You provoke
my dopest
ink crush

Pen poems
that will make
you peel
pants, panties,
and cause
your pubes
to blush

Shhh

Hush

I have
timeless flows

that will cause
**YOU** to flow

Even though
I'm 30
something

Age won't
play no role

Not in
your chemistry's
soft spot

I speak politely

My mind is freaky

Wondering

How can
I make
you love
lusting me?

*Heavenly
Hued Beauty*

*Cool Baby
Brown*

*Caramel*
*Queen*

*Cream*
*Complexion*

*Shaded*
*Mocha Bean*

A variety
of **AWESOME**
colors

They only
enhance
aureoles

Motivate me
to massage
mammaries
and nipples

Mouth marks
on massive ample
apples

Have a
matinee of
lip biting

Nails scratching
while love
fighting

**EXCITING**!

Moonlight hustle
with my
love muscle

Midday lustful tussles

All during
the day
dancing sexual

I make you
feel my
lyrical, physical

Now tell me

You enjoying
reading this
poetic visual?

# "Sideways"

(o)Watch(o)

--Love our peripherals--

...Legs
parallel
to pillows

Forming right
angles...

...Jah make
you make
intersections

Then I'll
enter your
section...

...We'll have
se[xxx]ssions

You'll be
sexing a
perpendicular
erection...

...Do

the math

Enter 10--->

...Now

subtract
a leg

...Add the
other to
a sturdy
shoulder

Numerous
strokes that
will multiply
and amplify
minor mumbles
into high
pitched cries...

**NO**
sounds
muffled

"*Jah got you moaning*"

...Our
carnal
journey

reaching
points of
eruption

Genitals
graphing
coordinates
to mutually
desired
destinations...

"Yeah...

...right there"

...Pelvic
thrusts
at high
speed
velocity

Lay on
your side
while I
straddle
your leg...

...You hold
the other

Another
25.4
insertion...

+ your
plush plump
protruding
mounds
sitting
sideways

= thundering
love claps

w/ invisible
strings of
lightening
rapidly
striking the
G Spot...

^Jump starting^

^Body jolting^

...Shallow
breaths being
the key
to faint
vocalized
elation's

Announcing
erupting
extremities...

...Together
we serenade
like well
pleased souls

"*I'm coming*"

## "Sexual Mathematics"

Position

*...facing me...*

Inversion

*...away from me...*

Division

*...part for me...*

Prepare for
an addition

Injection

25.4 centimeters
of insertion

1, 440 strokes
of rotation

Almost a foot
of continuous
penetration

Insemination

# **NOT** finished

10" inches
remain
embedded
for a
duration of
1 minute

Reverse 10"
inches, angle
downward,
then propel
forward 7"
inches in it

*Angular
thrusts*

Strokes to
the left
a decimal
of 0.500,
then right
6/12ths
of a
fraction

*Perpendicular
thrusts*

Strokes
upward
25.4 x 12
millimeters
before a
lengthy
subtraction

*Circular
thrusts*

Strokes in
a combination
of 180°
& 360°
degrees
of internal,
uninterrupted
action

*Numerous
thrusts*

Unaccountable
strokes that will
reconfigure the
uterus casket

I maneuver
my hips
in motions

that are
ecstatically
drastic

I maneuver
my hips
**SO** effortlessly
one would
think I
was elastic

I invite you
to experience
the act of
my sexual
mathematics

## "The No "E" Poem"

My cunnilingus
is astounding

I'll maintain
that you'll stay
**CONSTANTLY**
throbbing

Pulsating

Orally, I'm
stimulating

I'm **SO** good,
you would think
I caught you
in a labyrinth
of labia licking

You'll **KNOW**
my mouth organ
is captivating

Allow Jah to
worship your
womb piously

Lick your vulva
Satisfyingly

Carry out my
oral skills on
you gratifyingly

If your significant
individual shows
the inability to
lick you convincingly

Continuously shows
a sorrowful lack to
lick you ambitiously

Contact Jah with
your oral inquiry

I study cats
and hold a
PhD in pussy

So allow Jah
to lick yours
until you lack
**TOTAL** control
of your
muscular ability

Allow Jah to
lick you until
you orgasm

SO hard you
WILL walk
with difficulty

Truth is, Jah
WILL lick you
until you cum
SO hard it'll
handicap BOTH
your brain
AND body

And "*if*"
my oral skill
"*isn't*" working

I AM Jah

So I STILL
carry a 10"
inch monstrosity

I STILL own
the ability to
fill and thrust
CONTINUALLY

# "I'm Feeling Myself (*Touch Yourself*)"

I'm
the pundit

You're
my student

So broaden
your mental
horizons

Open for me

The time is
of no
consequence

Fill your mind
with thoughts
of me

It's as though
the concept
of tempo,
the concept
of gravity, the
concept of
being in this
existence you

have known,
has come to
a halt abruptly

Suddenly

You realize
that through
the interface
of your
fantasies and
dreams, an
understanding
is achieved

Truly, "*I*"
**MUST** be
**YOUR** muse,
in your quest
of being
entirely pleased

**OH**, the
pleasurable
possibilities!!!

Accompanied
with my
rhythmical
compositions,
you can be

even more
excited and
delighted with
the potentiality
of manhood

My lyricism
originates a
lasciviousness
yearning for
me that
brings you to
your **TRUE**
state of
womanhood

In all your
days of
longing, this
has been
the day
you long
for the most

For this
is the
day you
see yourself
for who
you are,

so if
I were
**YOU**, I
would
proudly gloat

Raise to
yourself a
physical
tribute, or
even self
indulging toast

Touch yourself
while being
taught the
course of
immeasurable
love by thee

Prolific professor
of poetry

**ME**!!!

A studier
of **YOUR**
cardiology

Dr. Jah, here
to fix your

heart with a
poetic remedy

And if required,
can perform
lyrical surgery

For
your anatomy

I can make
masturbatory
manuscripts

Or perform
a poesy that
will give you
an oral fix

Truth is

You're not even sure
it's me you love, but
you **ARE** so in love
with this scribes content

That you find
my name
floating across
your lips

...Jah...

You wish **MY**
lips were
floating across
**YOUR** lips

Wishing **MY**
hands were floating over
**YOUR** hips

Yeah, I'm
a trip for
writing this

I'm feeling
myself, so maybe I
seem a lil' arrogant

Lol... Yeah,
just peep how I
layer these verses with
a "*Kanye Treatment*"

But it **STILL**
doesn't prevent
you from wishing **MY**
lips were floating across
**YOUR** hips

Stopping periodically,

centrally, to take a
southern dip
and lick

**NO** man
you've **EVER** met has
**EVER** made you feel
like this

Just by
releasing verses

They
roll from
my tongue
and breach
your mental
fortress

Feel my
poetic forces

Have you
wetter than
a tsunami

Puffy your
punani

**TAKE THAT**
**TAKE THAT**
**TAKE THAT**
Mami

# "**Orgasm**"

We ALL seek penetrative waves

Determined to reach goals of oblivious ecstasy

Passion tangible with peak purpose

Dig... "If life is like a box of chocolates because you never know what you're going to get, then truth speak, I suggest you prepare for it by living outside the box..." ~ Jah X-El

## *Reflective Intermission 7*

Dig... {*Dear Mr. Balla...*} - "She **USED** you!?!? Dude... Truth speak, clever women find a need for foolish admirers who choose to communicate with money... No need to fault her for taking advantage of a lucrative opportunity... Commend her for utilizing her intelligence and teaching you a lesson... Consider it wisdom paid for!!!" – {*Dear Mr. Balla...*} ~ Jah X-El

# Chapter 7

# *Purposeful Penning*

## "Hate The Hate"

She hate you

Yet, she is
blessed
because
of you

Hate the
connection
she still
has to you

Yet she
would lay
down her
life for the
very being
which glues
her to you

She hate
the fear
that rises
in her throat
because of
the abuse
from you

But she
loves the
angelic child
that was
created with
the help
of you

And she
hates that
she doesn't
want to
share that
blessing
with you

She wants
to keep
that baby
hidden

Within the
safety
of her arms

Imprisoned

Away from
**YOU** and
**ALL** harm

## Secluded living

She hate
the hate
and the
vain
desperation
to have
a cordial
relationship
with you
that has
been forced
upon her

But she love

**OH GOD**,
how she
love the
child that
grew in her

In spite
of you

# "The One Night Stand"

Her eyes
find mine,
personalities align

Hearts chime,
crave climbs

2 dine,
1 enjoying cran,
1 enjoying wine

Perfect signs of
appetency combined

Lips emit shine,
from kissing so fine

Love is inclined,
surrendering, clothing
is resigned

Religion is declined,
as torso's grind

Oral exchanges applied,
bodies now entwined

Position reclined,

animal mimed

Her wetness primed,
genitalia aligned

...Tipple time...

My mouth imbibes
as she rides

Consume her

...My appetite is **NOT AT ALL** doused...

Then seize her

...Lil' Jah needs to be soused...

Then enter her
from behind

Her moistness guides,
my manhood glides

Annihilation from
my grinds

Decimation from
my slow wind

Vaginal dissipation
from inside

More thrusting implied,
early deposit tried

"**NO**!!!"

She replied,
my greed denied

Resistance supplied,
my erection survived

Ecstasy climbs,
she moans and whines

Joyous cries,
our climax' combines

Tensions unwind,
heartbeats decline

Snuggle time,
cuddling binds

Sleeping minds,
dreamy reminds

Morning finds

Us thirsting,
wanting to
be quenched
again, so let
us rewind

Concupiscence is a given,
that, we can underline

But you have a man,
I have a woman,
and I want us
to be enduring,
so our relationship
**MUST** be redefined

# "Sui Caedere"

...My
ending
will be
bittersweet

Below
the
Ambassador
Bridge, with
a memory
held and
caressed
by thumb
and tear...

...And
with the
echoes of
the world
surrounding
me

Waving
and flying
through, it
would be
with a
grin and

her name
leaving
my lips...

*"till later my love"*

...These
words
will mark
my reason

And
with the
day ending,
colors and
air kissing
my face
tenderly,
the night
would come
to fall
in as
the sounds
would
grow distant
and close
to the
moon's
melody...

...And

all that
**IS** would
be all
that **WAS**
and I'll
soon be
between
here and
home

*...there...*

[Wherever **THAT** is]

I
will
become
what we
**ALL** ponder
of...

Spirit

## "**Heroes**
### (*The Lie of Celebrity*)"

America is in
constant need
of heroes

Monolithic figures
upon which
the discontented
masses can
collectively filter
its praise

Someone deep
enough to feel,
yet not close
enough to touch

Whose lack
of commonality
makes them
the object
of adoration

Offering "*Plain
Jane's*" and
"*Average Joe's*"
temporary
departure from
the mediocrity

of their everyday
existence

Someone we
can look
up to
while they
look down
upon us

Pompous
aristocratic
egomaniacs

Whose
charismatic
rhetoric is
so overtly
redundant it
eventually
sounds
profound

Someone so
enthralled by
their own
celebrity it
makes them
completely
impervious to

the suffering
of others

Gods who
seemingly walk
amongst mortals

Immoral saints
who possess
potent powers
of persuasion

The slightest
glimpse into
their sexual
prowess could
evoke orgasmic
responses
amongst idolaters

Elvis
accomplished
this by
swiveling
his hips

Michael Jackson
did it
by grabbing
his crotch

The former,
was a
devout racist
who died
a slave
of his
own addictions

The latter,
before he died,
was a socially
retarded
pedophile
imprisoned by
his own demons
**AND**, as
it turned
out, **HIS**
own addictions

Yet we
exist in
a culture
where style
often
overpowers
substance

We rationalize

and justify
the behavior
of magnates

Trying to
convince
ourselves that
people who
have everything
are not prone
to bouts
of criminality

Yet human
nature tends
to defy logic

So **NO**
celebrity, from
the famous to
the infamous,
should be
allowed to
reside beyond
the realms
of persecution

We place
these iconoclastic
figurines upon
pristine pedestals

of perfection
Making it
possible for
an ex football
star and
a former
television
detective to
get away
with murder

Our need to
glorify cult
figures has
begun to
supersede
our conscience

We dress
them with
vestments of
piety and
righteousness
while they
repeatedly
prove
themselves
unworthy

Adorning then

with robes
of distinction

We perform
false coronations,
placing peasants
into the
thrones of kings

When we
reward
entertainers for
perpetuating the
negative
stereotypes of
sexually deviant
materialistic
thugs, it
becomes far
easier to
immerse
ourselves into
the role of
subservient
fanatic rather
than remain
disciplined
observers

Selling our
integrity, self

respect and
souls for the
opportunity
to live in
the shadow
of stars

Rather than
being content
with who
we are

But dudes
want to
be pimps

We're placating
ourselves by
pimping out
our rides,
and thinking
we're pimping
women, when
in reality,
simultaneously
we're pimping
out our minds

Losing our minds

And then seeking
leadership,
inspiration,
and trends from
the newest
celebrity find

**STOP** the
idol worship

Lusting over
paparazzi pics

Being led by
entertainers
disguised as
false prophets

Believing
media gossip

Because our
view of
heroism is
fueled by
star power

That's classic...

...Oxymoronic

Like the brave
being led
by a coward

# "Heroes" Pt. 2
## (*The Kwame Chronicle*)"

Justice!?

It's just **THIS**...

...A covenant when convenient

For celebrities, or those who carry that
prominence, for the most part, it's lenient...

...To see this, it **DOESN'T** take a genius

The law and legal system tend to favor those with
status...

...Which is why it astounds them **AND** "*Regular
Folk*" when they get punished for their
transgressions

...Truth speak, they deserved it

Just think...

...If it were an "*Average Joe*" they would get
thrown **UNDER** the prison establishment

As opposed to getting the ole "*Slap On The Wrist*"
treatment"...

...People **DON'T** want to hear this

They would rather blame the media...

...Or the "*White Man*" for crucifying public figures

"*He's black and he don't deserve it!!!*"

But reality is he made his own choices...

...Chose to listen to negative voices

Be influenced by skirts and Rolls Royces...

"*But Kwame was a victim!!!*"

...Naw, Kwame was an idiot

"*But Kwame is intelligent!!!*"

Yeah, and Kwame's
**ALSO** selfish **ALONG** with
possessing idiotic intelligence...

...No matter how much he was looked up to and
respected

Kwame doing what Kwame wanted while living in
a glass house means Kwame was stupid and the
opinion of outsiders were neglected...

...Carrying oneself in **THAT WAY**, a downfall **SHOULD** be expected

And they **SHOULD** go after him just like they **WOULD** do one of **US** if **WE** did the wrongs he committed...

...People, here's the lessons

**DON'T** let an ego trip prohibit your elevation...

...**DON'T** let satisfying your flesh stagnate your progression

And **PLEASE**, **DON'T** let greed supersede your blessings...

Dig... "Pride really **DOES** block blessings... **NO ONE** or **NOTHING** should prevent me from asking... **NOTHING** wrong with kneeling... Combined with hand clasping... Sincere praying... I could have **BEEN** receiving... Could have **BEEN** in position for God's gift giving... I'm **STILL** a work in progress, so this I'm **TRULY** realizing...... God, I thank you for your patience with me while I'm in the process of learning..." ~ Jah X-El

# *Reflective Intermission 8*

Dig... {*Do YOU*} - "Truth speak, trends tend to go in one year and out the other... That's why, as much as you can, make and follow your own..." - {*Do YOU*} ~ Jah X-El

## *About the Author*

***Jah X-El*** a resident of Detroit, Michigan, is a self-published author, poet, and spoken word artist that has performed, hosted, and co-hosted at different venues throughout the united states.

***Jah X-El*** is a man who writes from the perspective of trials, tribulations, and adversities encountered in his life as well as the varied experiences of others.

Jah's poetry is thought provoking, full of wisdom and compassion for both men and women alike.

After a successful first book, *Jah'sims - Inspirational Poems for Women,* Jah has allowed himself to continue to be a voice of wisdom and inspiration for women, as well as a catalyst of change by providing his words of encouragement and view on relationships, love, sexuality and politics in *Jah'isms II - The Variety Volume.*

190

19883424R00105

Made in the USA
Charleston, SC
16 June 2013